IMAGES OF ENGLAND

AROUND RAMSBOTTOM

IMAGES OF ENGLAND

AROUND
RAMSBOTTOM

ANDREW TODD &
THE RAMSBOTTOM HERITAGE SOCIETY

First published in 1995 by Tempus Publishing
Reprinted 2002

Reprinted in 2010 by
The History Press
The Mill, Brimscombe Port,
Stroud, Gloucestershire, GL5 2QG
www.thehistorypress.co.uk

British Library Cataloguing in Publication Data.
A catalogue record for this book is available from the British Library.

ISBN 978 0 7524 0356 4

Typesetting and origination by
Tempus Publishing Limited
Printed and bound in Great Britain by
Marston Book Services Limited, Didcot

Ramsbottom, looking east from Carr, c.1900. The Rising Sun beerhouse, Tanners Street, is
bottom left, with Carr Mill just beyond. In the centre foreground are Callender Street and
Rostron Road. The town centre is dominated by mill chimneys, the tallest (erected in 1890)
being that of Ramsbottom Paper Mills'. Over the Irwell, the Y-fork of Peel Brow and Bury New
Road climb the valley side to an undeveloped Shuttleworth. Park Chapel is top right.

Contents

Market Place, c.1900, looking west over Carr Street up to Rostron Road and Carr. Note the terrace with grocers shop at the corner of Central Street part of which was originally the pinners' workshop in Peel and Yates' Old Ground calico printing complex, possibly dating back to the 1780s. No. 3, next to the grocer's, was the town's public library from 1838 to 1919. By 1890 it was in a sad state, dismissed in one of the earliest editions of the local newspaper as no more than 'moths' food'! Joseph John Riley first produced his Ramsbottom Observer from 64 Bridge Street on 25 April 1890, but had since moved to the more imposing office, no. 9 Market Place, seen here. The newspaper, Liberal in sympathy, came out each Friday and cost 1d.

Introduction

The Ramsbottom Heritage Society has since 1987 collected some 2,000 photographs of the old Urban District. The following selection proves just how little the district of Ramsbottom has changed since 1895. There has been clearance of some town centre housing and modern infilling, several mills and churches have gone, the railway sidings are a memory; but the street plan, the main buildings and most of the original housing survive. The biggest topographical change actually occurred in the town's earliest days when the Grants transferred their calico printing from the Old Ground to The Square Works. Established by Robert Peel in 1783, the Old Ground was a complex of workshops in the area now encircled by Bolton Street, Bridge Street, Silver Street and Smithy Street and its removal allowed the growth of the modern town plan.

The story of Ramsbottom's pre-eminent family, the Grants, can be pieced together from our captions. Their impact is recorded in William Hume Elliot's *The Country and Church of the Cheeryble Brothers* (1893), a detailed book which also contains some of the earliest descriptions of the town. From starting operations at the Old Ground in January 1807 until the death of William in 1873, their influence on the life of the town was probably unchallenged. Unfortunately, much of the ink which records the family has been expended on the esoteric literary enigma of whether the brothers William and Daniel, who died in 1842 and 1855 respectively, were the prototypes of Charles Dickens' Cheeryble Brothers. (A more interesting debate has centred on the validity of their reputations as humanitarian employers and benefactors, challenged by the evidence of Ramsbottom Chartist, Peter Murray McDouall to an 1842 enquiry into the truck system.) Many other families and individuals have had big impacts – Peel and Yates can claim the earlier industrial connections, especially important at Summerseat whilst the Steads employed some 1,000 workers in six mills.

The doctrinal preferences of entrepreneurs and immigrant workers were reflected in the district's profusion of churches. Sectarianism spilled into education, since churches were the main providers of working class education until 1870, when elected local education boards could establish board schools to 'fill the gaps' in church provision, and make attendance compulsory. To preserve local monopolies, churches established new schools in a surge of building. In this rearguard action, they were assisted in the Lancashire cotton districts by the prejudices of the indigenous working classes who abhorred the prospect of their children being educated with the immigrant Catholic Irish. Perhaps this is why St. Paul's Church School was 'much enlarged' in 1870, and St. Andrew's opened in 1872 for 347 pupils. The Catholics opened St. Joseph's Church School on Lodge Street for 223 children in 1872, determined in turn that their children should not have to attend any board school, these nationally having quickly acquired a reputation for being 'unfit for the education of the children of the more respectable classes'. Of the handful of districts in England and Wales where no school board was needed, most were in south east Lancashire. The Ramsbottom school board was left with few gaps to fill.

A problem with constructing a district's history around a collection of photographs is that chance survival leaves important omissions. We have, for example, no photographs of Ramsbottom Mill, the earliest town centre spinning mill; nothing on Patmos Chapel or Christ Church; and no record of the vast railway sidings in which goods trains were marshalled for much of the cotton district. Another limitation of photographs is that they fail to record smells. Late nineteenth century Ramsbottom had many. There was just one main sewer, flushed periodically by Carr Mill lodge; an open sough ran down Carr Street from Carr Mill, an open sewer for human waste and refuse, only covered over by unemployed millhands during the 1860s cotton famine; the contents of the town's privies and ashpits were emptied onto a field of Samuel Kenyon's at Lower Fletcher Bank; urinals which stood in front of public houses regularly overflowed onto the streets; and notices had to be erected in 1868 ordering people not to throw 'ordure urine or offensive matter upon the streets'.

We have made reasonable attempts to establish copyright, but have accepted that in a town with a strong interest in its past, it is inevitable that many old photographs and postcards survive, their owners having little idea of their origin.

I must thank all those people who have deposited or loaned us prints, and the many Society members on whose recollections we have drawn. But I must single out Fred Entwistle whose numerous anecdotes whiled away so much of my time spent in our heritage centre. Sadly he died shortly before the proofs for this book were ready – I know how much pleasure checking them would have given him. I must also acknowledge the work of Brenda Decent and Barbara Park – the three of us spent so much of this record breaking, hot summer poring over prints and captions together at the Centre!

The Society's aim is to preserve and research the heritage of Ramsbottom and district, so we welcome the deposit of any documentary or photographic record. We meet monthly, and publish an informative heritage newsletter twice a year.

We can be contacted at The Heritage Centre, Carr Street, Ramsbottom, Bury.

Andrew Todd, Chairman, Ramsbottom Heritage Society,
September 1995

Acknowledgement

We acknowledge copyright of the *Bury Times* for the photograph reproduced on pages 16-17.

One

Town Centre
Market Place, Carr Street and Bolton Street

Roadworks in Market Place, in the first decade of this century. Note Joseph Matson's chemist shop, 1 Bolton Street – Jamieson Morton's until 1900, and Crawshaws' after 1913.

As well as hosting a market well into this century, Market Place was the town's meeting place. The largest gathering on record was the Chartist Rally of 1838, attended by c.5,000. Here, pre-World War I Whit walkers gather in the Place, probably for hymn singing.

Originally known as Four Lane Ends on account of the old roads which met there, Market Place has always been a natural place of departure. Here, the Ramsbottom Tradesmen's annual trip prepares to set off from outside the Grant Arms. J.W. Hutchinson & Son, who advertised themselves in 1928 as 'haulage contractors and charabanc proprietors', operated from Dundee Farm, on Dundee Lane.

Joseph Wardleworth's pork butcher's shop, 14 Market Place.

An early terrace, 'Irish Row', on Ramsbottom Lane, in the mid-1930s. This stretch of road was built in the late 1790s as a short cut from Market Place to Stubbins Lane. The old, pre-turnpike route north ran down what is now Bridge Street, left along Crow Lane and then along Stubbins Lane to Stubbins Bridge. This terrace was constructed on the new turnpike to house workers at Ramsbottom Mill, established by the Ashton Brothers of Middleton in 1802.

From Market Place, the old road to Bury ran west up Carr Street, to the hamlets of Carr and Foot o'th' Rake and then up The Rake to Holcombe. Carr Mill is at the end of the terraces. According to Hume Elliot, nos. 6 and 8 Carr Street (the centre houses in the four house terrace to the right) occupied the site of what was, in Old Ground days, the only well in the village.

The terraces shown above were back-to-backs, the rearmost houses fronting onto Back Carr Street, shown here. These were one-up-one-down, often rented furnished at around 4s 11d a week in the 1930s. Four outside 'tipplers' served the row of ten. Albert Street (known with its twin Victoria Street as 'Tory Town') is in the distance.

The same terraces on Carr Street viewed from the corner of Carr Mill. The nearest three, which appear on an 1806 plan of the Higher Ramsbottom estate, the earliest known map of the Old Ground, were probably some of the first workers' cottages to be erected in the village.

Back Carr Street – the variations in the heights of the terraces and the building breaks are evidence of the piecemeal construction of these modest houses. Their flagstone roofs and watershot stonework have more in common with the vernacular farmhouses of the area than with the standardised terraces erected in the later nineteenth century. Most of the Carr Street terraces were cleared by the Urban District Council in 1935, the empty site being visible in the view on page 2.

Whit walkers entering Bolton Street from Market Place in the 1920s. Note the trolley bus wires. Whitsuntide originated as a factory holiday in Manchester in 1801, as a rival attraction to Manchester Races! The custom spread throughout the cotton districts, being well-established in Bury by 1848, and probably in Ramsbottom soon after.

Whit walks on Bolton Street about the same period, a shot almost certainly taken by Harry Lonsdale from his Central Photographic Studio, just visible in the above photograph, at the corner of the third storey of Central Chambers. Different denominations walked on their own traditional day during Whit Week. The white dresses reflect the tradition which gave the festival its name – 'white Sunday'.

14

St. Andrew's 1909 Whit walkers passing The Flying Dutchman beerhouse (nos. 22–4 Bolton Street). This closed in December 1912. From 1835 to 1842, the Chartist leader Dr. Peter Murray McDouall probably practised medicine at no. 20, on the far side of the beerhouse. The Commercial Inn is just visible at the corner of Bolton Street and Market Place.

Tom Kay was a later occupant of no. 22, until c.1930. An electrician, his nameboard advertises Lighting, Power, Bells, Repairs. In the window are references to Hoover, Mazda Electric Lamps, Radiola Wireless sets, White Lamps 'for light without glare'. Note the mirror image of an illuminated advertising motif for 'Daniel Thwaites & Co. Celebrated Blackburn Beers'. 'You won't get a shock when you visit The Electrical Shop,' ran an advertisement of 1925. 'It's full of electricity, but the current is well under control – and so are the prices!'

A drab Bolton Street in the late 1970s, ten years before Ramsbottom became a tourist attraction. Apart from the large buildings in Market Place, there had been virtually no sandblasting. It was then possible to park on either side of the street.

A more leisurely age – a Bolton Street postcard with message dated 15 February 1914 shows a trolley bus approaching the cameraman (who has clearly set up near the centre of the street) whilst children saunter across towards the co-op stores. The Ramsbottom Industrial and Provident Society had opened its first store in Market Place in 1859, building these Bolton Street premises on the then fringe of the town. Opening in April 1863, the store had a massive 121' 9" frontage.

St. Paul's cubs on Bolton Street on their St. George's Day Parade, c.1968. This row succumbed to the 1980s property boom, most of the shops now being building society or other financial services branches. A generation will remember Frank Heys' large toy shop, now the National & Provincial Building Society. The Electricity showroom, like its gas counterpart opposite, was a casualty of a privatisation floatation. The ravage of the '90s has been fast food shops – planning permission for what had been the showroom to become a takeaway was refused in 1992 after a storm of local protest.

Regulars of the Clarence, Bolton Street, about to leave on a day trip, c.1930. Note that the group are posing in the roadway! Built c.1833 with a fine ashlar frontage, the hotel was one of the last in the town centre to retain traditional internal features, the bar, for example, dating back to the 1920s. Most of these were ripped out in Whitbread's 1988 revamp.

Looking up from Bolton Street to Albert Street, with Callender Street to the right. The slope, now landscaped, was known as Grants' Ground. These houses were demolished around 1960.

Callender Street was part of the traditional Whit walk circuits, judging from these views of New Jerusalem Church processions and above in 1911 and below in 1915, near the foot of Rostron Road. Carr Mill is visible to the rear. The substantial houses on Callender Street, many with bay windows, were erected in the 1860s and 1870s and were then some of the most fashionable residences in the town. The street's name derives from the calenders, used in the Old Ground to give 'face' to printed cloth. A calender house stood on the site of the present health centre.

Yates Bros Mill Furnishers and General Ironmongers, no. 41 Bolton Street, *c.*1910, display a great variety of goods both industrial and domestic. Note the edge of the iron wringer and ubiquitous tin bath for the Friday night family cleansing session. John J. Nuttall took over in 1922, under which name this business has traded ever since. This shop is one of the few in the town to have been involved in the same trade throughout this century. The following acrostic advertisement appeared in the *Ramsbottom Observer* early in 1903, and gives a flavour of the shop's stock:

YATES BROS' goods are the best in town
A nd those who buy them will never frown;
T o prove, just call and have a peep,
E verything is good and cheap.
S omething sure to please you'll see.
B uy it, try it, and satisfied you'll be;
R emember, 'tis a fact that's true,
O h don't forget to call and view.
T hey have ranges, fender kerbs and brasses,
H eating and cooking stoves, lamps and glasses;
E namel dishes, and frying pans,
R oasters, kettles and lading cans.
S aws and hammers, screws and nails,
I ron grates, pincers, and pails;
R akes, forks, garden shears, and spades,
O il bottles, fencing wire, and scythe blades.
N etting and felting, and galvanised sheeting,

M akers of which will want some beating;
O ven shelves, loaf, cake, and tart tins,
N uts and bolts, and flour bins.
G ood wringing machines, and window syringes,
E very description of locks and hinges;
R iddles, paving hammers and picks,
S hovels, fireguards, and candlesticks.
R azors, penknives and cutlery in cases,
A ugers, smoothing irons and coal vases;
M antles, wash leathers and window poles
S tepladders, clog irons, and shoe soles.
B rushes, and braces and bits, and tacks,
O il reading lamps and letter racks;
T ool chests, boxes, hooks and tiles,
T rowels, spring scales and files.
O bserve the address, 'tis Bolton Street,
M ay I tell you, wherever you buy, you'll never beat.

Two

Town Centre
Around Bridge Street

The Rose Queen procession passes Dungeon Row, Bridge Street in the early years of this century. The Suffragettes' dray is alongside George Johnson Cottrill's pork butchers shop (established 1866), nos. 40–2. Next door, to our left, is Harry Lonsdale's boot and shoemaker's shop, no. 38. Like most of the shops on Bridge Street and Bolton Street, Dungeon Row had been built in the early nineteenth century as workers' housing. The change of use on Bridge Street occurred gradually in the 1840s and 1850s.

There were over 20 public houses and beerhouses within five minutes walk of Market Place just before World War I. The Royal Oak, 37 Bridge Street, was built by the Bury Brewery Co. c.1897, on the site of an existing beerhouse. To the right is the Primitive Methodist Chapel, later a co-operative shop and employment exchange. Like many Ramsbottom beerhouses, the Royal Oak later expanded into its neighbour – in this case the grocer's shop at no. 35.

The upper end of Bridge Street was known as Water Street on account of the brook which, prior to being culverted in 1867, ran down its centre. In Old Ground days there were stepping stones near the site of the present Royal Oak. The bottom end of the street was always Bridge Street – a Crown Brewery dray delivers barrels to the Swan Inn, no. 20. Opposite is Wilkinson's, the tailors, at no. 23. Ramsbottom's trolley buses ran along Bridge Street from 1913 to 1925. This postcard was franked on 25 April 1916.

Less intoxicating drinks were to be had in the town's many eating houses and cafes. Numbers reduced in World War II when factories opened canteens to feed their rationed workers. Oswald Nickson's, 50 Bridge Street at the corner of Prince Street, was one of the classier cafes, catering for commercial travellers rather than millworkers. A sign of the times is that, this shop is now a 'takeaway'.

Joe Mercer's Station Temperance Bar, 7 Bridge Street, c.1900, opposite the Railway Hotel, and remembered for 'herbs, some herbal sweets and herb beer to be drunk on the premises'. Joe, renowned for his bowler, may be in the centre, surrounded by post boys, newspaper delivery boys and a railway porter. A favourite Sunday afternoon meeting venue for Ramsbottom and Shuttleworth children, it is now an Evangelical church. Catherine Cooper's confectionery shop is visible at no. 9.

Martin's Bank (now Barclays) was just two doors higher up than Mercer's. This block, erected in 1882 between existing buildings and numbered 9a–9d in consequence, had its upper storey removed in the 1950s, shortly after this shot was taken.

Bridge Street and the level crossing, about the same time. Note 9a-9d to the right. Ramsbottom Station level crossing was a source of constant friction between town and railway, and the subject of an 1893 parliamentary question to the President of the Board of Trade! Around 100 passenger trains, as well as goods trains and light engines, passed over it daily until the line's senescence in the 1960s. One solution, a subway, never materialised because the local board refused to subsidise its cost.

Ramsbottom's last toll bar, between the level crossing and Peel Bridge, was kept by John Grime and son Joseph, cloggers, for much of the nineteenth century. The site became the entrance to the Bridge Street Wharf riverside picnic area in 1994.

Peel Bridge, initially Ramsbottom Bridge, was built by Peel and Yates *c.*1789. It connected their calico printing premises, the Old Ground, with Peel Brow, the link road up to the Bury and Haslingden turnpike. The bridge remained the property of the owners of the Old Ground – the Grants after 1808. They and their successors charged tolls on vehicle traffic, 'for a long time a grievance to the people of Ramsbottom'. These rights, worth some £145 per annum by 1895, were bought out by the U.D.C., tolls being charged for the last time in October 1900. The gate's removal is recorded in a famous photograph reproduced by Ken Beetson in his *Ramsbottom Volume 2* (1978). The bridge remained unpaved until 1912.

Ramsbottom's original station was opened by the Manchester, Bury and Rossendale Railway on 25 September 1846. Once a busy junction station, with regular trains to Bury, Manchester, Bacup, Accrington, Burnley and Skipton, it had in its heyday a large staff, but ceased to be manned from 1968 following the closure of the Accrington and Rawtenstall-Bacup lines. During demolition in January 1971 the office was taken down by hand to retrieve the top quality dressed stone. Passenger trains ceased in 1972, but a weekly coal train continued to ply to Rawtenstall until December 1980. The 1908 view (below) looks north towards the level crossing and extensive sidings.

Railway Street during an, apparently, very good humoured General Strike, 1926. Note the goods shed and chimney of the Square Works in the background.

Opposite the station on Railway Street stood the Empire Picture Palace, built in 1910. This maypole dance may even have celebrated its opening. Owned by Blakeboroughs, the theatre closed in 1962 and burned down in 1978.

There were over a dozen butchers in Ramsbottom between the wars and advertisement phrases such as 'home killed meat only' or 'all our own killing' indicate that much slaughtering, especially of pigs, went on in the town. ('We could hear the squeals,' says an elderly former Bolton Street resident about one slaughterhouse off Square Street). Cottrill's pork butchers shop was on Bridge Street (see page 21) but the slaughtering was done at a discreet distance, on Kay Brow. Early this century, Daniel Grant's fine stable block (1825) was a sausage factory! Here the ingredients arrive at 'Cottrill's Works'.

The finished product on its way to the station. In the 1940s, the stables housed greengrocer John Dingwall's pigs, horse and cart and rabbits, the latter bred for pies, the skins being cured in Summerseat for gloves. This block became flats in 1994.

Lodge Street, off Kay Brow, commemorates John Gray's Lodge, one of the earliest in the town, extant in 1806, but drained in the 1970s and built over with flats. Gray was one of several Scots who lived in Scotch Row, now Scotland Place, once the Old Ground's dry house but converted to cottages when the Grants moved their operations to The Square Works. In 1911, the Amazon Lancers, a female dance troupe, prepared to leave Lodge Street to join the May Queen procession. St. Joseph's R.C. Church and school are to the right.

In the later nineteenth century, several engineering works and foundries were established close to the railway, particularly in the area between Square Street and Railway Street One specialism was the manufacture of tin plate, as at Richard Mason's, Prince Street, and James P. Nuttall's Palatine Metal Works, Palatine Street, seen here.

These metal workers and the town's many mill hands often lived in cramped terraces on or near the present Saturday market site. This view of early nineteenth century back-to-back housing on Silver Street looks north towards Bridge Street Squat and flag-floored, they were built in the same style as the Carr Street cottages shown on pages 12–13. Scheduled for demolition in 1935 (along with much of Square Street), all but the row on the right is still standing.

Some 300 people were employed at the Square Works, at the end of Square Street, the site of which is now T.N.T.'s transport depot. Archibald Hepburn had taken over 'The Square' from the Grants in 1867 and switched from calico printing to bleaching and finishing. Its chimney stands over the Square Works Sports Ground, seen here in the 1920s.

Looking west across Ramsbottom from above Bury New Road, c.1960. In the foreground is Ramsbottom Paper Mill, or Holcombe Mill, opened in 1857 by James Broadbent Ingham. It used old bagging, jute and manilla ropes to make casings and wrappings, but woodpulp, straw and rags for quality paper. The mill was often in trouble early this century for polluting the Irwell. Part of Trinity Paper Mills Ltd. from 1968 to 1995, it now belongs to the Danisco Group.

Workers at the Ramsbottom Paper Mill, c.1910. These men worked twelve hour day or night shifts to maintain continuous production, the norm in papermaking. The annual trip for the workforce here became commuted to a money payment. Workers received a day's wage prior to the August holiday.

New Jerusalem Church was opened by the spiritualist Swedenborgian sect in 1876 at the corner of Ramsbottom Lane, during the ministry of Rev. Samuel Pilkington. Their first chapel on the site, dating from 1831, is visible to the rear of the 1876 church. It has arched windows, and is built over two cottages. Samuel Ashton, co-owner of Ramsbottom Mill, was one of the first trustees. Soldiers were billeted here in World War II. By the 1960s the church was riddled with dry rot – it was demolished in 1971 and a memorial plaque placed on the site. Looking west across Factory Street, this view also takes in houses at the end of Heys Street, now Heatherside Road. This short street took its name from Henry Heys, the sometime local board chairman, St. Paul's churchwarden and owner of the nearby Victoria Mill. He also built the adjacent and elevated Carlton Place, its 1881 datestone bearing his initials.

The rear of the New Jerusalem Church, looking north along Ramsbottom Lane. The 1831 chapel, just visible, became the church hall once its 1876 replacement had been erected. The five-cottage terrace in the foreground had three storeys to the rear, where it faced onto Back Ramsbottom Lane.

The rear of the New Jerusalem Church is visible at the extreme right of this 1920 view north along Back Ramsbottom Lane. The three storey rear of the five-cottage terrace shown above is next to it. In the foreground is the row seen on page 11, 24 back-to-back houses sandwiched between Ramsbottom Lane and Back Ramsbottom Lane. Nine houses on this unsetted dirt track had just two cesspools and a privy midden between them, up to seventy yards distant.

A close up of the rear of the church, with Back Ramsbottom Lane's inadequate privies just visible on the extreme right. All these houses were demolished under a clearance order of 1935.

New Jerusalem's Day School occupied the basement of the church. The master (ie headmaster) George Washington evidently ran a tight ship – his class, Standard V, seem unusually well turned out, even for school photograph 'Sunday best'. The teenage girl and boy on the left will be student teachers, staying on after the normal leaving age to act as apprentice teachers until starting at training college at 18. The year was 1899. The school is known to have closed by the 1920s.

Like most churches and chapels in the town, New Jerusalem ran day and Sunday schools. Here, banner carriers pose prior to a Whit walk.

Crow Lane, 1928. Baby Edna Mary Holden is on the motorcycle as her father and uncle look on. Her more usual form of transport, an elegant coach-built pram, is parked beneath the window.

St. Paul's Church, Ramsbottom's first Anglican church, was opened in 1850 on the site of Crow Trees Farm. This typically frozen Victorian studio pose was photographed on Tuesday 24 September 1889 when the Church's changeringers rang the first peal of 5,040 changes. Back row, from the left: Abraham Clegg (bell no. 4), John H. Haydock (5), John W. Laycock (7), Jonathan Wolstenholme (3). Front row: John Tattersall (8), John T. Rostron (6), Henry H. Nutter (2), John Booth (1).

The Rev. W.H. Corbould, vicar from 1871 until his death in 1893, with the Church's Athletic Club (1891), inside St. Paul's School. He offended local traditionalists by making the church 'free' – ie removing rights to rent particular pews. 'The Church of England is the church of the people,' he wrote, 'and equality in God's House, is what they look for.'

Headmaster Henry Price posing with a class and its teacher at St. Paul's Church of England School, Crow Lane, in the 1890s. The school had originally occupied a pair of cottages, built c.1840 by the Ashtons of Ramsbottom Mill. The cottages appear to have doubled up as the town's Athenaeum, a kind of subscription-reading room.

Pupils and teachers in the infants school, 1910. Elementary schools provided mass education, modelled on factory production lines. St. Paul's had opened in 1868, and was enlarged in 1870. The infants school, seen here, was added in 1872 by William Grant, and a further extension in 1880 provided accommodation for 700 scholars. There are now about 85.

Another unusual St Paul's classroom view, *c.*1928.

Harvest time 1936. By this time, the school looks a little more pupil-friendly! Infants enjoy an apple with their breaktime milk. From the left: Harry Bardsley, Rodney Marsh (?), Vera Berry, Phyllis Brooks, Betty Mastines, Richard Beech, Ethel Smith, Doris Holden, Kathleen Sandiford.

Mr Price with his staff, in the 1930s.

Cricket has a long history in Ramsbottom. In the mid-nineteenth century, meadow land where the modern Saturday market is held was used for summer evening matches. Meadow land nearer the river around the site of modern Kenyon Street was also used. The modern ground at Acre Bottom may date back to 1866. Ramsbottom's Tradesmen's Cricket Team, who took advantage of 'Wednesday half-day closing' to play their games, stands outside the pavilion in 1896.

The Stead family of cotton manufacturers are credited with having established the Ramsbottom Club in 1845. James Stead was 'a very successful round-arm bowler'. Support from such influential and wealthy people, including the cashier J. Trego Gill, secured the club's future, and it was a founder member of the Lancashire League in 1892, the ground being one of the largest in this part of the county. Here, in 1937, a new roller (on which sits Mr. Greenhalgh) is presented to the club. Thomas Crawshaw is on the left.

Three

Carr, Holcombe and Holcombe Brook

Picnicking in the wood behind Carlton Place, Ramsbottom Lane, on Friday 14 August 1914.
The trees are visible in the background of the view on page 32.

Carr Mill and its chimney, as seen from the backyard of a cottage, possibly on Peel Street, behind the Grant Arms.

The interior of Carr Mill, also known locally as Devil Hole Mill, perhaps on account of the mill's sometime use of 'devils' – machines which tore up cop bottoms to reclaim the 'hard waste' cotton. The decorations are to celebrate the 21st birthday of the owner's son, Richard Nuttall, on 17 October 1913. In later years, Insulating Sleeves and Tapes Ltd. made electrical insulation here.

This area of Carr is now largely occupied by the big mid-1960s housing development centred on Carr Bank Ave. Prior to this, it was a well known beauty spot as can be seen in this view of Devil Hole Lodge and Rawcliffe's Field.

Carex Street in the 1920s from Springwood Street. The centre cottage, with hooded moulding over the ground floor window, was probably much older than its neighbours. This minute street led from Springwood Street, *behind* the houses into Spring Wood Mill yard and up to William Henry Birtwistle's Carr Oil Works, Ducie Street, owned originally by his step-father Samuel Porritt. This oil and tallow refinery (not seen in the view) operated from at least 1880 to 1965, and reopened as The Old Mill Hotel and Restaurant in 1967.

A view from Birtwistle's Carr Oil Works down to Spring Wood Mill (left), the mill yard cottages and Carex Street, of which the gable end is visible. Spring Wood Mill was built in 1842 and was acquired by the Porritts in 1845.

Carr Mill, first known as Magbrook Mill, was one of a series of early nineteenth century textile mills worked originally by the streams which dropped down from Dick Field Clough and Top Wood into Magbrook and supplied a series of lodges. (This is why some of Ramsbottom's early industrial housing was in the Carr and Kibb o'th' Crew area.) Like other early mills located in remote side valleys with good falls of water providing power, their locations left them obsolete when the economies of scale made large, steam-powered mills locate in towns, close to railways and workforces. Many of these water-powered fossils later eked out a living in the cotton waste trade, and when finally abandoned their rural positions meant that the unwanted sites were left simply to fall down.

This small clough (above) is still a 'graveyard' of early textile mills and their lodges. One of the oldest was Top Wood or Higher Mill, a fulling mill with tenter ground possibly built about 1710, judging from an auction advertisement of 1778. It stood within the crescent shape of its lodge, nearest the camera. Below the next lodge stood Kibb o'th' Crew or Lower Mill. The chimney of Spring Wood Mill is to the right. Top Wood Farm is to the left.

Demolished in the late 1940s and one of the most prestigious addresses in the town, Carr Bank House, was built in 1850 on the site of Carr Barn Farm, for John Grant of Nuttall Hall, who did not live to occupy it. His son William lived there for a time. Later residents included William and Henry Stead, and Dr. William Deans who used Carr Bank Lodge on Ramsbottom Lane as his surgery c.1900. There were fine grounds, with a half-moon shaped moat round the house where kingfishers darted for fish. St. Paul's Whit walkers remember reaching Carr Bank by the back drive, off Springwood Street, and receiving oranges.

The Victoria Carriage at Springwood, 1891. The passengers are Mr. A. Porritt and Mr. N. Townsend. Bond is the coachman and Prince the horse. The exact location of this spot is unknown.

A postcard, franked July 1914, of Holcombe and Foot o'th'Rake from unprepossesing allotment sheds behind Victoria Street. The field in the foreground, now infilled with post-war housing, was called Tanner Croft. The footpath running straight across it, still traceable in parts amongst these houses, emerges at Tanners, alongside the modern barn conversion. Its other end started at Grant Entry, by Spring Cottage on Bolton Street. Directly under Holcombe Church stands its rectory, whilst The Rake drops at 1 in 4 from Holcombe village to the cluster of houses known as Foot o'th'Rake. From there, running under the top third of the view, is a very rural Dundee Lane.

Rake Fold c.1910. The Rake is to the right of the wall. The lamp standard, still insitu, was made at Joseph Strang's Prince Foundry, Prince Street.

An early twentieth century shot of the much photographed prospect of Chapel Lane and Holcombe Village which immediately faces anyone with enough energy to crest the summit of The Rake. At the top of Holcombe Hill (1,100 ft) is Peel Tower, in height (128 ft), and erected at local expense in 1852 to commemorate Bury-born Sir Robert Peel (1788-1850). His repeal of the protectionist Corn Laws in 1846 suited both millowners and workers in the cotton districts.

A view back down Chapel Lane, about the same time, towards Emmanuel Church, rebuilt in 1852-3. The terrace behind what may be the local postman on his round is nos. 2-18 Helmshore Road. It was built around 1820 by the Holcombe Friendly Society of Printers, a terminating building society established by calico printers to finance this housing project. Opposite is Holcombe Church of England School.

Children in the street outside the school celebrating the Relief of Mafeking in 1901, during the Boer War. World War I affected the school directly when a German Zeppelin scored a direct hit. Note the north end of the printers' terrace to the rear. Beyond are other houses built on Chapel Lane by their society, *c.1823*.

A later view of this stretch of Helmshore Road, showing the school, printers' houses and the commanding location of Emmanuel Church overlooking Ramsbottom.

The Holcombe Hunt, dating back to 1617, is one of the oldest packs of harriers and has strong associations with Holcombe Village. John Jackson (1835-1905), Huntsman to the Holcombe Hunt from 1867 to 1899 is seen with hounds, presumably, at their Holcombe kennels. In Jackson's time, the huntsmen ran on foot with the hounds, and he boasted that he 'could run any mon i' Lancashire'. The hounds were kennelled in the village from at least 1772 until their move to their present site at Brandlesholme between the Wars. Locals recall whole horse and cow carcases being carted down the narrow track which led from the Shoulder of Mutton to the kennels in Tagg Wood.

The Holcombe Hunt in the 1920s, by the Shoulder of Mutton in Holcombe village.

John Jackson, with hunting horn, at 'The Last Wakes Monday in Holcombe', believed to have been about 1880. The August 'Wakes-time' at Holcombe was, in the early years of the last century, an occasion for illegal cockfighting at the White Hart Inn. A secluded village, without a police constable, such events attracted the gentry from as far away as Manchester and Bolton. Bare knuckle fighting matches were staged in the road and assaults were common, not to mention the quaint art of 'grinning through a horse's collar', staged on the green in front of the White Hart. They 'pood faces horrible enoof to ma' one's belly wartch'. The Rev. George Nightingale, incumbent from 1849-75, is credited with expurgating the village of these idiosyncrasies!

On 24 May 1902, two large stones were transported from Fletcher Bank Quarry in Shuttleworth to Holcombe Moor, and erected as a monument to commemorate the medieval Pilgrim's Cross, the surviving socket of which had been vandalised the previous August. One of the two teams of horses, owned by Whittakers, wheelwrights and blacksmiths of Edenfield, is seen here by Higher House, Moor Road. This early eighteenth century building served as the White Hart Inn until 1884. It stands opposite the village's other inn, the Shoulder of Mutton, formerly known as 'the Lower House'.

The Manor House, Cross Lane, *c.*1910, built by the Rostron family about 1794. Holcombe has a concentration of such large buildings, a reflection of its importance prior to the emergence of Ramsbottom as an industrial town. Until the construction of the turnpike road from Bolton to Edenfield in the late 1790s, for example, the only two inns in the Ramsbottom district were at Holcombe.

About 600 yards along Moor Bottom Road stands Hey House, the grandest mansion in the area, containing carved woodwork reputedly from Whalley Abbey. Built by Robert Browne in 1616, and occupied by his family until the mid-nineteenth century, Hey House later belonged to members of the local textile elite such as Thomas Gorton and the Steads.

Hey House overlooks Redisher Wood, where this Edwardian group is picnicking by the Holcombe Brook. Many local people remember 'lemonade and jam butties on hot summer days' in the '20s and '30s, whilst electric trains brought many trippers to the nearby Holcombe Brook station. Postmarked Ramsbottom, this postcard was sent by Susan Booth, who lived at 37 Bolton Street, to Cissie Stevenson of 161, Stubbins Lane on 8 September 1903. 'I will be down at St Pauls Church, watching Mr Bracewell's wedding Tomorrow. So be their and if it is fine we will walk on to Bury after,' it reads. The postcard was published by bookseller Thomas Holden of 16 Bridge Street.

A Ramsbottom trolley bus at the Hare and Hounds, Holcombe Brook, *c.*1920. The main road to Ramsbottom, Bolton Road West, was constructed in the late 1790s, whilst Lumb Carr Road, forking left up to Holcombe, followed c.1812. The inn was probably built shortly afterwards, the new turnpike junction having become a prime site for a hostelry.

Opened in 1898, Holcombe Brook Post Office occupied part of the late eighteenth century building at the corner of Longsight and Bolton Road West rebuilt in 1990 as Holcombe Mews. The station building is just visible to the right. The Post Office moved to 9 Longsight Road in April 1915, but is now further down the road, by Garden City. No. 9 is currently Harrison's Estate Agency.

Ramsbottom Urban District Council toyed with the notion of introducing trams for 10 years, but was deterred by the prospective expense of tracklaying, widening Peel Bridge and building tramsheds. A majority of its electorate, polled specially in 1913, opted for trolley buses, and seven of these 'trackless trams' were eventually bought. The first two arrived from the Rail-less Traction Co. of Leeds that August, and the service began on Thursday the 13th. This is an early shot of two buses outside the Hare and Hounds (note Great War army uniforms). The rear antique may be one of the August 1913 couple. The later models were more comfortable – nos. 5 and 6 (1915) were 'beautiful to ride in', and 'like being in a motor car'. All, however had solid rubber tyres, and much of their route was on setts. 'You used to step off them and you'd be shaking!' one man remembered 60 years on.

Same location, a few years later.

The funeral cortege of licensee John Forshaw waits outside his inn, the Hare and Hounds, prior to the final journey up Lumb Carr Road to Holcombe Church. A gravestone there records that he had died on 26 March 1887, aged 79. Forshaw's son, John, had married Amelia, daughter of John Spencer, owner of the Hazelhurst Engraving Works. The business is now owned by their great grandson John Spencer Forshaw. Note partial setting of road, and part constructed wall, since removed.

Four

Summerseat, Nuttall, Nuttall Lane, Dundee Lane and

Half a mile down the Holcombe Brook stood water-powered Robin Road Mill, Summerseat, photographed c.1910. Peel and Yates were successful calico printers at Bury and Ramsbottom, thousands of domestic weavers supplying them with cloth. Robin Road (c.1780) was one of their five Summerseat spinning mills which provided the yarn. Weaving was the last process of cotton manufacture to be automated, the adoption of the power loom causing the famous riots of April 1826. Richard Hamer, the then owner, had thirty eight power looms destroyed at Robin Road on the 26th. Note the ten 'tied' cottages facing the mill. The typically pre-1860 square chimney is evidence of an auxiliary steam engine.

Joshua Hoyle's Brooksbottoms Mill, looking north west across the Irwell from near Cragg Farm in 1900. One of Peel and Yates' spinning mills stood here, the site later being acquired by John Robinson Kay, an archetypal paternalistic Victorian entrepreneur and philanthropist. Joshua Hoyle and Sons Ltd. were a Bacup firm who had acquired Kay's mill through the marriage of Isaac, son of Joshua Hoyle, to Mary, daughter of John Robinson Kay. The Hoyles promptly demolished the mill and opened this one, the fourth on the site, in 1876. Built in a fine Italianate style from sandstone quarried at Fletcher Bank, the mill employed as many as 400 people in its heyday. It closed in 1978, and Bury M.B.C. proposed its demolition, raising an outcry – 'the most significant building in the conservation area', opined the Victorian Society. A £1.5 million scheme to save the riverside portion was agreed, the chimney was demolished in 1984, and the present conversion to studio apartments and flats was completed in 1985.

Opposite: Brooksbottoms Viaduct on the East Lancahire Railway cuts Summerseat in half. In the foreground are the Brick Houses, ten rows of houses built in 1885 to accommodate employees of Joshua Hoyle's Brooksbottoms Mill. By 1968 the houses were in very bad condition and as each became vacant it was bought by Ramsbottom U.D.C. and bricked up. In 1985 Bury M.B.C. demolished six of the rows, to providing extra space and light for the remaining refurbished houses. At the south end of the viaduct is the goods warehouse, now flats, whilst above stands the unusually gothic Rowlands Wesleyan Chapel, built in 1847 and demolished in 1978.

Twist Mill, Summerseat. The site was used by Edward Hamer in the eighteenth century to spin yarn for fustian cloth. Bought by Peel and Yates in 1786 to supply their outworkers, the mill was sold off in 1812 as the firm withdrew its operations from the Ramsbottom area. Purchased by its manager Richard Hamer, it passed to his daughter Mary, wife of John Robinson Kay who already owned Brooksbottoms Mill. The view is from a postcard franked 'Summerseat 5.10.05'. In the background are Upper Mill (left) and Robin Road Mill, seen on page 57. Note the backyards behind the brick terrace, and Twist Bridge to the right of the mill.

Walking west from Twist Mill, this was the view along Railway Street c.1920, the brick houses to the left being those visble at the top of the previous page. The older terrace on the right was Long Row, believed to have been built c.1795 to house pauper apprentices brought by Peel and Yates from city workhouses. It was demolished in 1965.

The quaintly named Lovers Walk ran alongside a mill goit from Railway Street to Wood Road. Franked on 16 Jan 1908, this postcard of Susan Booth's thanked her friend Cissie for a Christmas gift.

Chest, or Chase Wheel Bridge – the collapse of a parapet in 1968 led to a dispute as to whether this link across the Irwell to Wood Road hamlet was a private road. An estate map of 1785 established its status as a public highway, and Greater Manchester Council effected the repair, putting in metal railings to replace the parapet.

Upstream at Brooksbottoms, the cobbled Water Side ran from the Brick Houses, visible in the background, to Robin Road. Two girls are standing by the Irwell, *c*.1910.

Walmersley House, built in 1847 for John Robinson Kay. It opened as the Robinson Kay Home for Incurable Gentlewomen in 1886, having being presented by his daughter Betsy to the trustees of the Northern Counties Hospitals for Incurables as a memorial to her parents. Later a nursing home, it opened in 1995 as Highbank, a rehabilitation unit for young people with head injuries.

A Bury train emerges from Nuttall Tunnel in the 1960s, heading south to Summerseat. The tunnel, just 115 yards long, was an unnecessary feature of the 1846 railway, dug at the insistence of John Grant of nearby Nuttall Hall to protect his view. Diesel sets were introduced on the Bury-Bacup service in February 1956, running until the line's closure to passengers in June 1972.

The quickest route from Summerseat to Ramsbottom is over Brox's Brow to Nuttall, and generations of clogs must have rattled over its cobbles down to Brooksbottoms Mill. At the Nuttall end, the track became Starling Street, known locally as Shepsters, or Shebby Row, 'shepster' being the dialect for starling. These eight houses stood next to Nuttall Hall Farm, and are shown during demolition c.1940.

Nos. 2-12 Nuttall Road, abandoned about the same time. Writing in 1893, Hume Elliot quotes people in the village remembering the first half of the nineteenth century as a time when it was 'busy, thriving, populous' with three mills. The decaying chimney of the last to close is visible in the view on page 63.

5

Jim Welding, last manager of the Ocean Chemical Co., outside his home, 17 Lower Nuttall Road, the last surviving house in Nuttall Village, and formerly the company offices. He died in 1991, aged 92, and his house soon became a vandalised ruin.

The Ocean Chemical Works, extant from 1921-52 in the valley bottom between Nuttall Village and Nuttall Bridge, was rarely photographed, and these views show why! It produced alkali for local bleaching and printing works and chloride of lime for use in paper making, in swimming baths, Bird's Custard and Yorkshire Relish. It also enjoyed the sinister distinction of being the only cyanide making plant in Britain, this initially being its sole product. One first hand account of the Norwegian-owned plant's activities makes it sound horrendous. Lime lakes were spawned, sodium gas was burned off to provide four foot flare lighting and the workforce took on a yellowish tinge, whilst unburned hydrogen was released into the atmosphere. Locals commented on its 'horrible smell'. Ocean Chemicals, October 1928, looking south west from Nuttall Bridge through some sickly trees. Note the crenellated Nuttall Hall Farm beyond.

Opposite: Note the mass of barrels, and their cavalier storage. There was no lifting gear. 'My brother had started at Ocean Chemicals . . . it wasn't unknown for him to come home with his hands bleeding from contact with the chemicals.' A crude metal gauze with cotton wool centre was the only facial protection. The hourly rate was 1s 1d in the '30s, and a week's holiday at half pay was only secured when unionisation took place at that time. There was also shift work, since the alkali plant worked 24 hours a day.

From the Nuttall side. These photographs were taken by the company, hence the superimposed numbers identifying key buildings such as towers and settling tanks.

The interior of the cyanide manufacturing plant, which closed in 1931. The cyanide was heated in nickel pots, using the firm's own gas, and packed into sealed steel drums. Used in steelmaking, it was exported to the U.S.A., South Africa and New Zealand.

Lorries seen in the works yard, September 1928. Access was via Nuttall Lane, along which all the chemicals travelled, some of it on horse drawn trailers.

Only yards north of this environmental horror was the charmingly located Nuttall Bridge. Referred to as 'th'owd bridge' in the early nineteenth century, it carried over the Irwell an old east-west packway, linking Bury Old Road at Pinfold, Shuttleworth, with Holcombe, via Nuttall Lane and Dundee Lane. The bridge collapsed on 16 November 1928, and has been replaced at different times by two rather less attractive footbridges.

Just over the bridge, stood Nuttall Hall, built in 1817 for John Grant (1775-1855), brother of the 'Cheeryble Grants'. Grant had bought and demolished Lower Shipperbottom Farm to provide a site for his mansion.

Purchased by Lt. Col. Austin Townsend Porritt, the hall was in 1928 donated along with 15 acres of land to the people of Ramsbottom to become Nuttall Park. The house was demolished in 1952, only the Hall Cottages (visible to the left on the top photograph) survived.

Part way along Nuttall Lane stands the Aitken Memorial and Jubilee Cottage Hospital, seen here shortly after its opening on 13 November 1899, complete with ten beds. Ramsbottom's first hospital had been provided by Mrs May Aitken in 1896 in a modified house on Dundee Lane, and the recovery of her husband from serious illness that year prompted her to found the entirely new hospital shown here. Queen Victoria's Diamond Jubilee of 1897 was also commemorated in the hospital's name.

The Cottage Hospital, with convalescing soldiers outside, during the Great War. Other large buildings had to be drafted into use as military hospitals – Stubbins Vale House, for example, received its first batch of wounded soldiers in October 1914.

Gala Day at Ramsbottom Cottage Hospital, July 1919, with Miss E. Hand, matron since 1914, in the centre.

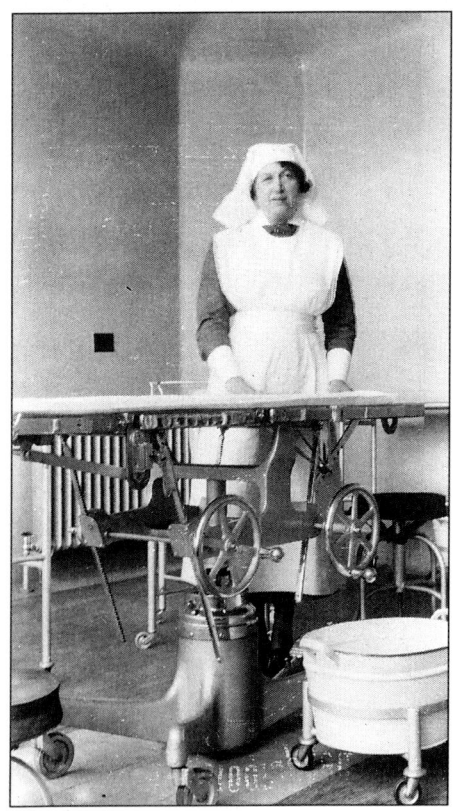

Miss Hand's successor, Matron Lees, stands in the state-of-the-art operating theatre, opened in 1937.

The opening of the operating theatre and children's ward, 1937. Front row: Capt. Richard Porritt (killed by a Stuka at Seclin in the Dunkirk campaign), Mrs. Porritt, Lt. Col. Austin Townsend Porritt J.P. (of The Cliffe, Stubbins). Middle row only Mr. Barlow (2nd), Sidney Castle (3rd) and Matron Lees (far right) are known. Back row: Thomas Sutcliffe, -?-, Dr. Hugh Lawrie, William Fenwick, -?-.

A later photograph of the staff of the Cottage Hospital. Back row, from the left: Nurses Pilling and Gough, -?-, Sister Smith, -?-, Nurse Barcroft. Front from the left: Thomas Sutcliffe, Dr. Charles William Crawshaw, Matron Lees, Miss Hand, Dr. Hugh Lawrie (the U.D.C.'s medical officer of health) and Sidney Castle. Other doctors who acted as medical officers here around this time were Ralph Crompton (chauffer-driven from his home at Carr Bank Cottage down to his surgery by the Council Offices in Market Place) and Henry George Deans.

Hazelhurst Council School, on Geoffrey Street, c.1905. It was erected in 1903 by the Walmersley and Ramsbottom School Board, on land bought for £550 from Mary, widow of Geoffrey Grime Wild of Higher Barn, Holcombe. Accommodating 368 children, it was placed under county council control under the 1902 Education Act.

St. Andrew's Church School, c.1933. Front row, from the left: Billy Almond, -?-, Norman Lingard, Jack Brown, -?-, Ralph Porter. Second row: Hilda Smith, Ena Boardman, Olive -?-, Joyce Boardman, Joan Savin, Dorothy Webster, Ethel Tattersall, Enid Farnworth, Mary Hankinson, Eve White. Third row: -?-, Bernard Ward, Freda Hargreaves, Mary Farnworth, Mary Wardle, Dorothy Dane, Dora Harrison, Rex Wadsley, Eric Finnerty, Billy Dane; back row: Jack Heaton; ? Hamer, -?-, Jack Schofield, Bill Snow, Eric Sergenson, Vincent Lees, -?-, Clifford Walsh.

St. Andrew's staff, a few years earlier. The seated figures may be Miss Martha Hutchinson, infants' mistress, and William A. Bracewell, headmaster. Standing is James Haslam, a stalwart at the school until 1945, and best remembered for introducing Gilbert and Sullivan to the children. He was deputy organist at St. Paul's Church, and lived in Callender Street.

Like St. Paul's, the parish church was also a focus for sporting activities, in this case running. St. Andrew's Harrier's, c.1898. Back row, from the left: Robert Birtwistle, James Thornton, George Heap, Albert Sutherst, James Diggle, Robert Callister, Fred Ashworth, Robert Dewhurst, John Almond, Arthur Ashworth, Sam Avery. Middle row: William Barlow, Charles Walker, Howarth Clegg, William Mayor, James Farrel, Wilfred Cook, Walter Walker, Harry Fogg. Front: J.W. Hutchinson, Robert Chew.

Opposite: St Andrew's Anglican church, Bolton Street, built 1832-4 by William Grant, the elder of the two putative 'Cheeryble Brothers' as a memorial to his parents. Its initial connection with the Presbyterian Church of Scotland explains the faintly Scottish appearance. Many Scots, drawn to Ramsbottom in the last century, possibly in the wake of the Grants, are buried in its small yard. Inside are memorials to the many Ramsbottom Grants who lie in vaults under the church.

The Cheeryble Brothers' heir was their nephew William Grant. Educated at Eton, and perhaps with social pretensions, he was a high Anglican – his ejection of the Presbyterian congregation in 1869 and transfer of St. Andrew's to the established church caused a local furore and, very nearly, a violent confrontation! A major refurbishment in 1993-4 cost £110,000 – over twenty times the building's original cost. In the process, the quatrefoil stonework visible in the window at the foot of the tower was removed in one piece and buried in the churchyard for possible reuse in the future. Note the famous clock, powered by a 29 ft 6 in pendulum (one of the longest in the country). It was made at The Square Printworks by John Buchanan, the Grants' engineer – he is commemorated in the name of the nearby street. In recent years, the tower has at times also accommodated barn owls and kestrels.

Views of Dundee Lane, towards Holcombe Church, before road-widening encroached into these gardens. Above: From the junction with Shilton Street, *c.*1900. (Postcard published by T. Holden, 16 Bridge Street) Below: Nearer to Dundee Independent School (note signboard on left), from the junction with Charlotte Street (Postcard published by Robert Smethurst, a bookseller at 47 Bridge Street in the 1920s.)

DUNDEE LANE, RAMSBOTTOM.

Dundee Lane looking in the opposite direction, the School House to the right. Between 1914 and 1939 brick terraces were built (in stages) on the left hand side of the lane. This shot, taken *c.*1900, records the then open view to St. Andrew's Church, just visible left of the trees.

Joseph and Sarah Walker outside the School House, c.1900. Mrs. Walker was almost certainly the lady who related its history to a journalist of the *Bury Times* in 1893. Built in 1664 in Holcombe churchyard as Tottington manor courthouse and parish school, it was superseded in its latter function by the erection of the Church Schools on Helmshore Road in 1864. Ellis Howarth bought the structure for £11 and carted it down to its present site. The stone carvings came from Manchester Cathedral and/or Clitheroe. The School House was originally known as Well House, on account of the well at its front which served local residents until the mid-1920s. There were many wells or 'spouts' in Ramsbottom – a lot can still be traced, but often only as rubbish-filled recesses in roadside walls.

79

Dundee Presbyterian Chapel, Dundee Lane, opened in 1712, sold with its adjacent manse in 1976 and demolished in 1978. Occupying the site of chapel and graveyard, the manse garden now has the distinction of having 12 gravestones lining its walls, including that of Rev. Andrew MacLean, minister here from 1830-4, before he and the congregation removed to William Grant's St. Andrew's on Bolton Street. On being ejected in 1869, the congregation returned briefly to this chapel until their new St. Andrew's was opened in 1873.

Upwind of Ramsbottom's chimneys, several substantial stone houses were built in the Barwood area of the town in the late nineteenth century, the homes of various doctors, clergymen and industrialists. Barwood Mount is the five house terrace on the right whilst beyond stands Hope House and Rose Hill Primitive Methodist Chapel (opened 1889, demolished 1949). On the left is Samlesbury House (once the Christ Church manse), at the corner of Buchanan Street. Only Spring Terrace (beyond), built in the 1830s, and Barwood House Gatehouse predate the regularising of the incline of the road in the nineteenth century, and their foundations are well below the present carriageway.

Bolton Street c.1900 and the other St. Andrew's in Ramsbottom, built by the ejected congregation on the corner of Kay Brow above Barwood Lee at a cost of over £7,000 in 1872-3. Known as St. Andrew's (Dundee) Presbyterian Church, and perhaps the most imposing of the town's churches, it was demolished in 1926, the tower being transferred to English Martyr's Catholic Church at Whalley Range, Manchester. Only the yard wall survives. In the foreground is the original c.1853 portion of the Major Hotel. St. Joseph's R.C. Church is in the distance. The shot was taken from 'The Green', a popular play area for local children.

Garnett Street, shown on this postcard franked 27 August 1917, is the next side street off Bolton Street after Buchanan Street. Built in the 1880s in pitch faced stonework, it is typical of much of the quality terraced housing built on the fringe of the town centre in the late nineteenth century. The name commemorates three generations of a notable family of architect/builders. Christopher Garnett was recruited by the Grants from Lancaster in 1821 and he supervised the construction of The Square calico printing works (1821-2), Barwood Lee stable block (1825), Grants' Tower (1828) and St Andrew's Church (1832-4); James, his son, built Park Congregational Schools; and John, James's son, was responsible for the rebuilding of Christ Church, Market Place (1874) and for Holcombe Hall (1910) as the Aitken Sanitorium. John was an early resident of Garnett Street, living at no. 12 on Gladstone Terrace, built 1885.

Five

Shuttleworth and Edenfield

Looking west down Peel Brow towards Ramsbottom in the 1950s. Laid out c.1789 to link the town with the Bury and Haslingden turnpike, Peel Brow in the 1850s was described as 'more like the bed of a stream, and almost impassable for vehicular traffic'. The photographer is immediately above the Eagle and Child Hotel, on Whalley Road, Shuttleworth.

An inter-war view of the Eagle and Child Hotel, colloquially known even as late as the 1980s as 'Top Bunk'. The lone figure is presumably the landlord. Note the promotion of mild beer at 5d a pint, and the bus timetable on the wall. The hotel became the Beau Vallon restaurant in 1990.

An earlier licensee was George Ormerod. His wife Hannah was nicknamed 'Missus o' th' Bunk'. 'Bunk' came from Bank Lane, the old name for the main road through the village.

Bury New Road was built c.1835 by the Grants, Ashtons and Duckworths, the latter owning Shipperbottom coalpit, probably on Whitelow Lane. The stretch overlooking the valley floor was colonised later in the century by a series of impressive mansions – Irwell View, Irwell Mount, Riversdale – the homes of the town's dignitaries, one of whom is seen seated in his chauffer-driven saloon outside Hawthorne.

The road was intended to provide an easier gradient than that on Peel Brow, but the sharp bend by Park Cottage (seen to the rear) was the scene of accidents such as this, when a horse drawn lorry crashed into the garden at the corner of Nuttall Hall Lane. This postcard was franked January 1909.

Hume Elliot records that there were 'no houses east of the river in Old Ground days'. Much of the building has taken place since the 1930s. Peel Brow Council Estate and new prefabs are visible across the centre of this post-war view, again taken from behind Whalley Road.

Peel Brow and the small streets fanning off it were the earliest housing on the valley's lower slope (see view on page 4). Most of these stone terraces were built at the end of the last century by two local stonemason/builders, Thomas and James Foster. Spring View, on Eliza Street, appears on this postcard postmarked July 1902. Perhaps building was not yet completed, for on the terrace's datestone is the year 1903.

The Ashworth family, having just moved into a brand new house, no. 5, on an as yet unmetalled Fir Street, c.1890. Such narrow courses of pitch faced stonework were typical of this later period of terrace building. The atmosphere generated by hundreds of domestic coal fires and factory furnaces would soon render this pristine honey-coloured local sandstone the characteristically sooty black. Note the new venetian blinds. The family had evidently dressed in their Sunday best for the photograph.

The rear yard looks just as fresh. Note the rougher stonework in comparison with the frontage, a common contrast in Ramsbottom terraces. Annie and Harold pose for a photograph with their toy horse!

As a consequence of all this building, the Walmersley and Ramsbottom School Board opened Peel Brow Board School in 1901 to accommodate 600 pupils. After 1903 it came under Lancashire County Council control as Ramsbottom Peel Brow Council School. An early headmaster, George Cheshire, is commemorated by the name of a nearby modern court. Renamed Ramsbottom County Secondary School, it closed in July 1979.

Senior pupils (probably the oldest in the school) at Peel Brow in 1904.

Peel Brow School from the corner of Whalley Road and Peel Brow. The M66 extension was driven through the site in the late 1970s, and Peel Brow now passes over the motorway here on a large bridge.

The national school leaving age was raised from twelve to fourteen years in 1918, and it was no longer possible to teach all pupils in a single 'elementary' category. Secondary and primary were separated by law after 1926. At Peel Brow, this was achieved by partitioning and extending the existing building. Infants were already provided for separately. Here, 1935 infants pose with uncharacteristic formality in the Play Room. The junior and secondary schools shared the same building until the 1976 opening of the present junior school on Fir Street. Secondary pupils transferred to Woodhey High School after closure in July 1979.

'Bottom o' th' Bye Road' is the core of Shuttleworth village and stands at the bottom end of 'the Croft', the narrow, industrialised valley of the Cross Bank Brook which drops down from Turn to the Irwell. Bye Road forms a loop off the main Bury to Haslingden turnpike (seen to the left), its name implying that it was the original line of road through the village. The open space in front of the terrace, Edith Street, was the site of Top Mill. The gable end of St. John in the Wilderness Church (built 1847) is visible in the background.

Peace celebrations outside Bank Lane Baptist Church School, 1919.

One of Ramsbottom Urban District Council's new Thorneycroft T-type petrol buses, pictured outside the Duckworth Arms in 1923. The switch to petrol was a response to the shortcomings of the Council's fleet of trolley buses.

One of Shuttleworth carrier Fred Stringfellow's lorries in the late 1920s. 'Any distance catered for,' claimed an advertisement of 1928, no easy task with solid tyres and only oil lamps to guide the vehicles through winter fog and snow. The load of drums is from Kay's soapworks, Kenyon Street, Ramsbottom. Stringfellow's garage was on Whalley Road.

Two vanished landmarks from each extremity of Shuttleworth – in the south stood Grants Tower (left) erected in 1828 on Top o' th' Hoof, reputedly to commemorate the site off Bury Old Road from which in 1783 the Grant family first saw Ramsbottom. It is now remembered by local people as a favourite pre-War summer venue. It cost 2d to climb the spiral stairs. 'On special days Mrs Turner had an old tramcar in the field above the swings and here sweets, pop and ice cream were sold.' Repairs were neglected in wartime, despite early use as a Home Guard post. The inevitable collapse came on 22 September 1944, and there are countless 'sole witness' tales in the district about that afternoon. Wartime rumour insisted that the tower was purposely demolished to prevent the Luftwaffe using it and Peel Tower as dual landmarks to guide them to Manchester. 'The whole tower collapsed,' said an eye witness at Bent House Farm, 'and huge clouds of dust poured down the hillside into the valley.'

At the north end of Shuttleworth, the Scout Moor Colliery Co., owned by Lawrence Duckworth and his descendants, leased this single shaft coalpit from the Earls of Derby for much of the last century, together with mining rights under 160 acres of the moor. The coal was taken down to New Gate in Turn Village on a half mile tramway, the trackbed of which is still visible. The workforce included women and children in its early days, and subsequently about six men. Acquired by the Whittaker family, it closed in 1941, reopening unsuccessfully in 1952. It was derelict by 1955, the approximate date of this view.

Dearden Brook marked the boundary between Shuttleworth and Edenfield, and was heavily worked by textile mills. Bridge Mill was built *c*.1824 by Richard Rostron ('Pinch Dicky'). It was damaged by rioters in April 1826 and twice by fire before being rebuilt and expanded by Alexander Barlow and Sons after 1879. In 1894 it became the first mill in the district to be lit by electricity. The line of the Edenfield – Rochdale road, built in the late 1790s, is marked by the wall.

A few hundred yards downstream stands Eden Wood Mill, run by John and James Rostron as early as 1818 for cotton spinning, and later used by Turnbull and Stockdale as a dyeworks for their famous 'Rosebank' fabrics. Run now by Edward Turnbull, Eden Wood is one of only two places in England where traditional hand block printing is still carried on.

Two views of a Ramsbottom U.D.C. trolley bus at Market Place, Edenfield, c.1920.

Looking north from Market Place along Market Street, during the Whit walks. On the left are W. Elton, butchers, at 7 Market Place, and Haworth's Refreshment Rooms.

One of Ramsbottom's earliest trolley buses at the route's northerly terminus, c.1920, with Edenfield Church of England Elementary School in the background. This close up reveals that the wheels of this bus look suspiciously as if they are made of solid wood! Note also the setts over which most of the route from Holcombe Brook ran – hardly surprising that the buses spent much of their lives having new springs, bodies and wheels replaced in the workshops!

Market Place, Edenfield – the record snowfall of February 1940. 'There were amazing reports of drifts up to 15 feet deep at Holcombe and of all the roads into Ramsbottom being blocked, with cars and even buses buried in some of them.' Note the survival of the trolley wire standards, despite the last trolley bus having been withdrawn in 1931.

A stranded petrol bus, likely to be a Ribble, at the Rostron Arms, Market Place, probably in the winter of early 1947. Wilsons Ales of Newton Heath, Manchester, on sale.

Despite standing at an uncomfortable and isolated 875 ft, just off Gin Croft Lane half a mile to the north east of Edenfield Village, New Hall was a centre of domestic weaving at least from the seventeenth century. This early sixteenth century house was the home of a cadet branch of the Rawstorne family of Lumb Hall from 1538 until its purchase by Bury and District Water Board in 1906. Part of the abandoned building survived into the 1970s. Note the range of mullioned windows in the east wing, and the characteristic Rossendale raised centre lights in the west wing.

Ewood Bridge, Near Edenfield

Also at the northern end of Edenfield is Ewood Bridge, where the 1789 Bury–Haslingden turnpike crossed the Irwell. The East Lancashire Railway built an isolated railhead of a station here, the nearest point on a main road to Edenfield. A horse drawn butcher's cart is visible. John Parkinson had a spinning mill at 'Heywood Bridge' in 1833, and the site may have been used for calico printing earlier. The mill was partly demolished in the 1950s.

A 1920s postcard of Bolton Road North, published by A. Johnson of Edenfield. In the late nineteenth and early twentieth Centuries, postcards were used to communicate with people only short distances away, performing the modern role of the telephone. Consequently, local photographers, stationers and booksellers produced a profusion of postcards of anything of remotely local interest, from news events to portraits of local dignitaries. Even a trolley bus labouring up from Stubbins towards Edenfield was evidently considered eventful! The absence of any car traffic helps to explain why in 1917 an average of 10,000 passengers a week had been carried by the U.D.C.'s fleet of six buses. Note the new council houses to the right, and the clear view to Stubbins Congregational Church uninterrupted by the roundabout later to constitute the south end of the 1968 Edenfield by-pass. Holcombe Tower has been 'touched up' to make it more prominent, a common practice amongst postcard makers.

Six

Stubbins and Stubbins Lane

The Edenfield and Little Bolton Trust's turnpike road, built in the late 1790s, crossed the Irwell at Stubbins Bridge, seen here from the footpath to Strongstry in 1928. The field to the left of the river, playing fields since 1923, was the scene of the famous Chatterton Riot of 1826 in which several thousand loombreakers defied thirty one soldiers and attacked Aitken and Lord's factory. The view, looking south east, also takes in Turnbull and Stockdale's Croft End Bleach Works.

The winding room at Turnbull and Stockdale's Chatterton Weaving Shed, 1949. Spun thread (seen in the foreground on spindles) is being prepared as warp, ready for the looms. The mill was erected in 1908, as part of a policy of 'vertical expansion' at Stubbins – concentrating virtually the entire process of textile manufacture in one village.

Rosebank Printworks, bought in 1896, was the first Stubbins acquisition by the Stacksteads calico printers Turnbull and Stockdale. Printing may have begun here in 1804, and by 1831 the works was operated by Jackson, Watson and Greig, calico and quilting printers. The earlier buildings are visible to the right. Stubbins Congregational Church (1867) peeps above the newer building.

A closer view of Croft End Bleach Works, taken from the same spot as the top shot – near Sheep Hey Farm. Turnbull and Stockdale bought the works in 1900, as part of their Stubbins concentration programme. Known initially as New Bridge Bleach Works, it had also been run by Jackson, Watson and Greig in the 1830s.

The 'Black Set' – Turnbull and Stockdale's maintenance men at Rosebank Printworks in the early 1920s. The firm had a workforce of about 750 in 1931, and about 1,000 by 1951. Benefits included the use of a nine hole golf course between the Duckworth Arms and Eden Wood Mill, and a progressive sports club with two football and eight cricket teams, two of the latter being for women! Workers tended to stay with the firm – £25 was awarded to anyone clocking up 25 years, and in 1931 there were 128 employees who had done so. Turnbull and Stockdale's recipe for success was (1) weaving their own cloth and printing their own designs for the Rosebank Fabric range supplied to the furnishing trade and (2) commission printing Manchester trade customers' cloth. Many of their designs were used in the Cunard Liners and Prince Philip had the Queens Navee design in his study. The company began to decline in the 1950s, and was taken over by Sandersons in 1964. Rosebank continued to produce goods until a takeover by the Reed Group in 1967 when printing ceased. Edward Turnbull, great grandson of founder William Turnbull, has maintained family and craft continuity with the firm's early days, retaining traditional handblock printing at Eden Wood Mill.

George Henry Charnley stands outside the offices at Rosebank, early this century. Note the basket, used to collect the cans in which workers received their wages.

A Turnbull and Stockdale wagon carrying an advertising display in the 1920s.

Porritt & Spencer's workers at Stubbins Vale during the General Strike, 1926. These employees, presumably, were willing to work, and with buses at a standstill had to be brought to the mill in the company's own transport.

The Winding Room on the 'cotton side' of Porritt & Spencer's Stubbins Vale Mills, possibly on the occasion of George V's Silver Jubilee, May 1935, or of George VI's Coronation in 1937. Porritt Brothers and Austin had started at Stubbins Vale in 1851, making woollen and cotton cloths for calico printing and paper making machinery, together with 'all descriptions of endless machine felts'.

A Festival of Britain float on a British Railways truck at Cromptons' Stubbins Paper Mill, 1951. This site has a long industrial history – Thomas Sandiford built a calico printing works here some time before 1818, later run by William Rumney as an engraving and calico printing works. Cromptons took over the factory in 1911, making paper for cigarette manufacturers throughout the world. Fort Sterling now make toilet rolls here from recycled paper.

Before the nineteenth century industrialisation of Stubbins shown on these pages, the sparse population eked out a living from farms such as this at Buckden Clough, augmenting their income with some domestic textile production. This tributary side valley of the Irwell was part of the 435 acres of land known as Stubbins Estate given to the National Trust in 1943 by Lt. Col. A. T. Porritt in memory of his son Capt. Richard W. Porritt killed in action at Seclin in France in 1940.

Rather more characteristic of industrial Stubbins – local people pose with an array of chimneys, terraced houses, motley allotments and outhouses as a backcloth. Neither the identity of the group nor the occasion are known.

Industrial housing on Dale Street, parallel to Bolton Road North, Stubbins – the occasion is the 1937 Coronation of George VI. The older portion of Rosebank Printworks is visible beyond the Irwell.

The same celebration, but looking in the opposite direction towards Cuba Mill, where Turnbull and Stockdale had its quilting department. The mill was burned down, probably deliberately, in 1974 and the site is now occupied by the Cuba Industrial Estate. Dale Street commemorates John Dale, manager at Union Mill, which stood in the same yard as Cuba Mill.

The great bulk of Ramsbottom Gas Works, with offices at its entrance on the east side of Bolton Road North, Stubbins. Established in 1854 by the Ramsbottom Gasworks Co., the works had four holders with a capacity of 520,000 cubic feet. The company remained independent until the U.K. Gas Corporation took over the 'Gas Works and well appointed offices and showrooms' in 1936. After nationalisation in 1949 the works closed, but the offices were opened up quarterly so that bills could be paid. When demolished, the rubble from the huge Cuba Mill chimney was used to infill the gasometer sites.

Houses for the mill foremen – the original village of Stubbins, centred on Stubbins Street, is on the west side of Bolton Road North. These five substantial cottages, known as Stubbins Vale Terrace, dominate the street. They were built by the Porritts in 1871 at a cost of £1,440.

At its junction with Stubbins Street, Bolton Road North emerges from under the fine skew railway bridge to become Stubbins Lane. This spot has flooded regularly for as long as anyone can remember. Here, a horse appears to be rescuing a stranded car from a Stubbins Lane flood in 1928/9.

The Aitken Memorial and Jubilee Cottage Hospital had opened in 1899 (see pages 71-4). An endowment fund was formed to support it and other district nursing funds. The Cycle Club in Ramsbottom was active in raising money for the charity, organising an annual Rose Queen Festival. This was also known as the Cycle Parade, although no bicycles were involved! Sunday schools, day schools and local industry took part with decorated floats, collections being made along the route. Here, the 1908 parade passes the string of coalyards sited along Stubbins Lane for transhipment from the railway sidings onto the sort of carts shown on this photograph. J. Morris & Co.'s is in the foreground. Their offices were in Silver Street. Behind the telegraph pole is 'the Flock Mill' (now Holcombe Sheet Metal/Hardman's Engineering) where cotton waste-filled pillows and mattresses were made. Beyond is Victoria Mill and then the gasworks. The skyline is dominated by the stone Cuba Mill chimney, the massive base of which is visible in the Dale Street view on page 108. Local wisdom had it that a horse and cart could have been driven around its top!

The Victoria Mill, Stubbins Lane, after the fire which gutted it after World War II. Ironically, it is now the site of the fire station. Ramsbottom's extensive railway sidings were to the rear.

Ramsbottom's launch into automated public transport in 1913 necessitated the construction of sheds to house the new fleet of trolley buses. Their heavy repair costs persuaded general manager Sydney Parsons to phase in petrol buses as replacements from 1922 onwards. Here, the new fleet stands outside the sheds c.1923. The bowler hatted gentleman will be Mr Parsons. Some 1840s stone cottages are visible on Stubbins Lane to the rear.

The older part of the sheds accommodated the trolley buses. Note the horse drawn vehicle to the left, with gantry for wire maintenance. The operation was always referred to as the Ramsbottom U.D.C. Tramways (hence the stone tablet) since the trolleys were technically 'trackless trams'.

A bus at the same Stubbins Lane depot, painted in Air Force blue to raise money for the war effort during War Wings Week, 1941. Third and fourth from the right are Ebenezer Nightingale and John Bradley. The site of the sheds, originally part of the lodge powering the Ashtons' Ramsbottom Mill, was cleared in 1991, the present Esso garage being erected the same year.

Just 400 yards along Ramsbottom Lane and we are back in Market Place, seen here shortly before the present gardens were laid out by Ramsbottom U.D.C. and 'the Castle' built in the early 1950s. William Grant lived at Top o' th' Brow, renaming it Grant Lodge after buying it and the surrounding Ramsbottom estate from the firm of Peel & Yates for £9,800 in October 1808. The house, which forms the rear portion of the present Grant Arms, became a hotel in 1828, after which the present frontage was added. The Conservative and Unionist Club was built in 1860, and was given to the U.D.C. in the late 1950s to become the Civic Hall.

Seven

People

The 'Empire Children' await the opening of the picture house on Railway Street. This could have been the initial 1910 opening, judging by the costume. Saturday Matinees were a part of many children's weekly routine – in 1928, the Empire and Royal jointly advertised for parents to 'send your children on Saturday Afternoon when we will give them a Good Show and afford them every care'. Admission was 3d for the under twelves.

A family wedding of Kays the soapmakers. The marriage of Tom Kay to Eve Sutcliffe took place on 30 March 1907 at the Dundee Independent Sabbath School. Tom, born 1880, was in the Royal Navy at the time. Immediately behind the bride are his parents Alice (nee Dale) and John Kay. Children of John and Alice are marked in this list with asterisks. Back row, to the right of John, Eliza*, then Margaret Ann Davenport (John's sister), Thomas Davenport (her husband), Rhoda Dearden, Albert* (later to marry Rhoda). Middle row, from extreme left: Nancy Rodgers (John's sister, seated), Herbert (John's brother) and wife Elizabeth, Tom Rostron Kay (another brother) and wife Esther. On the ground, at the front: the boy kneeling second from the right is Carswell*, who was killed in the Great War, whilst sitting to his right is Margaret Kay*. Tom Rostron Kay and brother Herbert began soapmaking on Shilton Street in 1884, supported financially by their sister Margaret Ann, and trading as James Kay and Sons. The firm moved to its present Kenyon Street site c.1900. Herbert's son, James was the last Kay managing director when a management buy-out took place in 1951.

Another eminent local family – the Porritts, relaxing with friends in summer sunshine on the lawn at Green Mount, Stubbins, in the mid-1890s. From the left: Joshua Townsend, Kate Porritt, Richard Millett Porritt (her father, owner of Green Mount), his wife Sarah Jane, and Dr and Mrs Sidebottom.

The Petch Brothers of Summerseat – the nine pictured here (there were 11 in all) served in the Army, Navy, Home Guard or Fire Service during World War II and returned to civilian life unscathed. Back row, from the left: Alex, Albert, Arthur, Jack and Sidney. Front row: Alfred, John, William and Thomas.

Churches and their schools offered a wide network of social contact. They acted as a focus for that range of spare time activities which have today become secularised into sports clubs and leisure centres. Here a group of 18–30s, or the like, are on a 1928 charabanc outing on the Isle of Man.

George Edward Warner (1882-1947) of Nuttall Lane was a slater, and like many tradesmen went to some trouble to advertise his business in the annual Cycle Parade. This photograph was taken near his Nuttall Lane yard to celebrate his prize-winning float. The white card on the horse's collar, which the Heritage Society has in its collection, reads: 'Ramsbottom Rose Queen Festival, Cycle Parade, Trade and Tradesmen's Demonstration, Saturday July 16th 1910, First prize Class 6, Best display of Local Industries (on Cart or Lurry).'

Mr Beswick (right) with the Ramsbottom Co-op cart ready for the same Rose Queen procession. The dressing table and wash stand on display were probably the very latest design. The children appear more interested in the camera.

The visit of the 1934 Lancashire Cotton Queen to Dundee Congregational Church. In 1931, the *Daily Dispatch* launched the Cotton Queen competition to help reverse the industry's decline after its loss of markets during and after World War I. Lancashire millworkers chose a queen for their own mill. Town finalists were sent to Blackpool's Tower Ballroom and the Cotton Queen for the year was chosen by *Dispatch* readers. Dressed in model gowns, she sought through visits, speeches and 'photo-opportunities' such as this to raise the status of cotton from a workaday to a luxury commodity for middle class women.

A class from Holcombe Church of England School *c.*1930. Primary schools catered for rather more pupils than today – Holcombe was actually something of a minnow with places for only 252 in 1925! This class of thirty three must also rate as small for the period. Mechanistic teaching methods were an inevitable result of teachers being seriously outnumbered! Holcombe had opened on 8 January 1865, at a time when elementary education was neither free nor compulsory. Pupils were 'half timers', twenty six attending in the morning, and another twenty six in the afternoon. School attendance only became compulsory in 1880, although part-time schooling continued for many children over the age of ten. There was much local opposition in Ramsbottom to any attempt to end the 'half time' system. Full time attendance only became compulsory nationally in 1918.

Tower City football team, 1908-9 season, with the eponymous Grant's Tower to the rear. Photographer T.A. Smethurst's captioning is not clear! Back row, from the left: W. Avery, J. Dewhurst, F. Haworth, J. Higginbottom, D. Bramoley, H. Jeffries. Middle row: J. Barlow, J. Reynolds, S. Lawton, H. Dykes, H. Duckworth, S. Schofield, T. French, J. Robinson, W. Smith. Front row: J. Nuttall, H. Greenhalgh, W. Battersby, A. Smith, A. Henderson, P. Labron, J. Avery.

A 1920s portrait of the Rose and Crown bowling team, taken by Ramsbottom photographer W. Lingard. Tom Sutcliffe, proprietor of the billiard rooms on Smithy Brow (now known as Smithy Street), stands to the right in the light suit. Behind the bowling green is the roof and chimney of Spring Wood Mill, and beyond those the woodland of Carr Bank.

A studio portrait of one of the town's billiard teams, in the 1920s. Seated, from the left: -?-, James Kay (president), George Savin (captain), Riley Tonge, -?- McKinley, William Baldwin. Standing: John Oldfield,-?- Kay,-?- Haworth, Tom Loughlan, W.E. Hamer, Tim Maddacks, ? Foster, William Moore, William Maden and Tom Entwistle.

Finally, portraits of various well known local people. Possibly the earliest Ramsbottom resident to have been photographed – James Bassett was the town's last bellman and town crier, with a voice reputedly audible on Holcombe Moor, some 500 ft above Market Place! He would hawk cockels and mussels between shouting news or 'crying a lost child'. 'A kind hearted and lovable old man and fond of children, and the children loved him,' he was one of the first pauper apprentices to be carted up from city workhouses to work in Ashtons' Ramsbottom Mill – reputedly, his name derived from Bassett Street in London where he had been found. Despite such modest origins, he was well respected in the town, and a substantial crowd followed his coffin up to Holcombe Churchyard, where he is buried. This portrait is the only glass photograph in the Society's collection.

Ramsbottom could erupt into spectacular violence – there was a railway navvy riot in 1846 – yet the town's police presence in 1851 was just one sergeant and a constable. In the 1868 general election campaign gangs of partisan colliers and quarrymen wrecked their opponents' meetings. At the Athenaeum (now St. Paul's School) it was 'a not infrequent spectacle … to see a man's head pushed through one of the squares of glass'. Extra police were drafted in to impose peace by parading the streets with drawn swords. Nuttall, in contrast, must have been a peaceful spot – it was not until c.1900 that the Lancashire Constabulary established a presence. Fred Whiteside, the village's first policeman, poses in a photographer's studio in his best uniform. He was killed in World War I.

Ramsbottom's official 'knocker up', c.1900 – In the days before alarm clocks, Mr. Robinson would tour the town's streets with a pole, rousing its workers with a tap on the door or bedroom window.

Richard Barlow (1865-1943), Ramsbottom postman from 1882 to 1925. His regular contacts with townspeople prompted him to maintain a chronicle of local events, mostly deaths, from about 1900 to 1940. The contents range from the newsworthy ('20 Oct 1918 Sunday – Fire at St Andrews Church, Ramsbottom. Estimated damages £2,480') and the domestic ('23 Jan 1920 New centre gas bracket fixed at 35 Dundee Lane') to the personal ('24 July 1924 R. Barlow bitten by a dog at 48 Kenyon Street').

Ramsbottom's other great chronicler, author of the town's only local history, William Hume Elliot. Pastor at St. Andrew's (Dundee) Presbyterian Church until 1907, Hume Elliot arrived at Ramsbottom in December 1874, five years after the 'ejectment' crisis. His great work *The Country and Church of the Cheeryble Brothers* (1893) set out to record, in detail, the circumstances of the 1869 ejection of the St. Andrew's congregation and the subsequent litigation. Despite arguing adamantly that William Grant had been wrong to seize the church and convert it to Anglicanism, Hume Elliot was a fawning adulator of the latter's uncle, William, who had built St. Andrew's for the Presbyterians in 1832-4. The book catalogues much of the Grant family's connection with Ramsbottom, and is also the town's first oral history project in that it contains an account of the Old Ground, no more than a 50 year old memory in Hume Elliot's day.

For thirty years before the creation of Ramsbottom Urban District Council in 1894, the district was governed by Ramsbottom Local Board. It is probable that this photograph, taken by an Ollerton photographer on the occasion of an outing, for some unknown reason, to Sherwood Forest, may be of its members. Some of those named were serving on the U.D.C. in 1896-7. Many were local businessmen. Back row, from the left: R. Leeming; E. Hardman; J. Haworth; John Garnett of Springfield, architect; Henry Lees Sladin of Hazelhurst, ironmonger on Bolton Street; J. Ashworth; S. Holden of Holcombe; J Brooke; John Keenaghan, wine merchant and tobacconist on Bridge Street. Middle row: G. Whitaker; R. Lee; T. Moore of Whalley Road; J. Brooke. Front row: John O. Haworth, a Square Street pawnbroker; John W. Barlow of Riverside, Bury New Road, solicitor; William Bentley of Rose Villa, Bolton Street, slater; J. H. Raikes.

BIRD'S-EYE VIEW OF RAMSBOTTOM.

A final overview of Ramsbottom and Shuttleworth, looking east from above Carr *c*.1900. There must have been few days in the year when the atmosphere was clear enough for such a photograph. Perhaps it was during the July wakes holidays, when the mills shut down. Square Works, however, visible on the extreme right, is definitely smoking, as may be others. Legislation attempted to limit pollution by insisting that black smoke could only be emitted for a certain number of minutes per hour. The *Ramsbottom Observer*, however, was frequently scathing about the 'gingerly half hearted' enforcement by the local board of this law. Contrasting this with the tougher enforcement in Manchester and Salford, the paper suggested that the board acted in the interests of the manufacturers – enforcement, it declared, in a wry 1890 parody of the millowners' defence was a 'socialist' policy, likely 'to hamper the great industries of the neighbourhood'. One consequence was the great winter smogs which would settle in the Valley for days at a time – in December 1890 the *Observer* reported how its artist had been delayed in executing views for the new year almanac sheet because 'the ever present fog has for some weeks past rendered the work of sketching accurately very difficult'! Note the narrowness of Bury New Road, the early stages of exploitation at Fletcher Bank Quarry, the allotments and coops on waste land now infilled with modern housing and Grants Tower on Top o' th' Hoof, top right.

Index